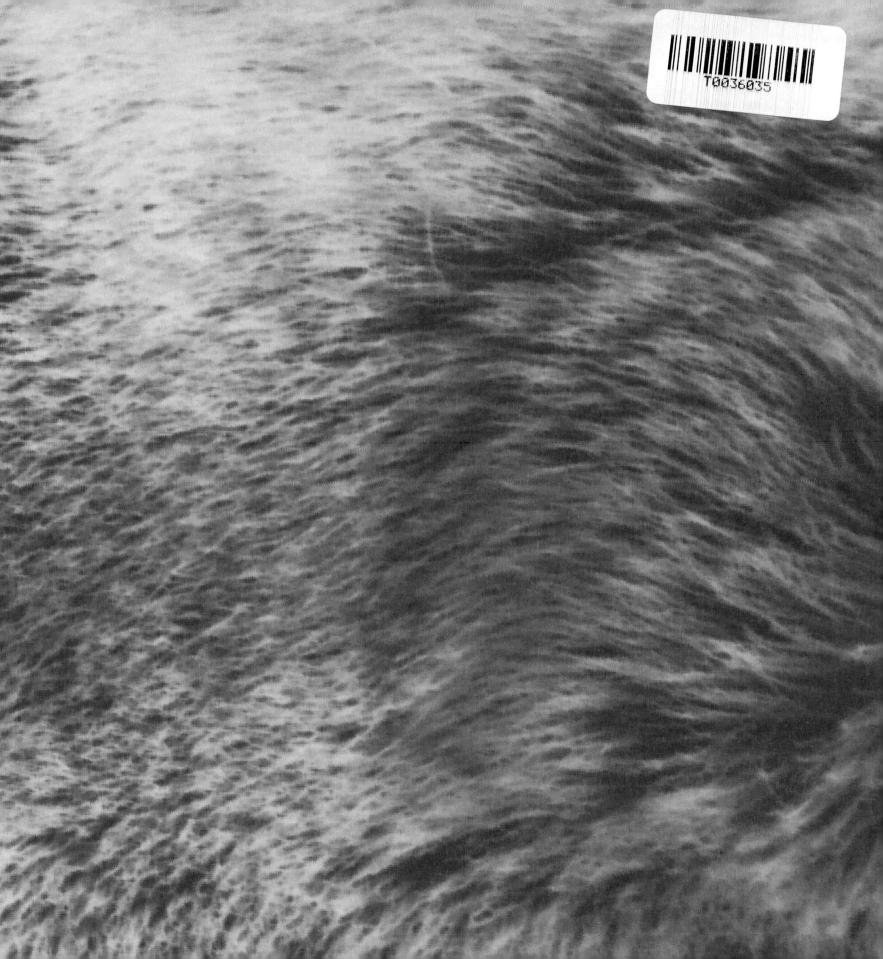

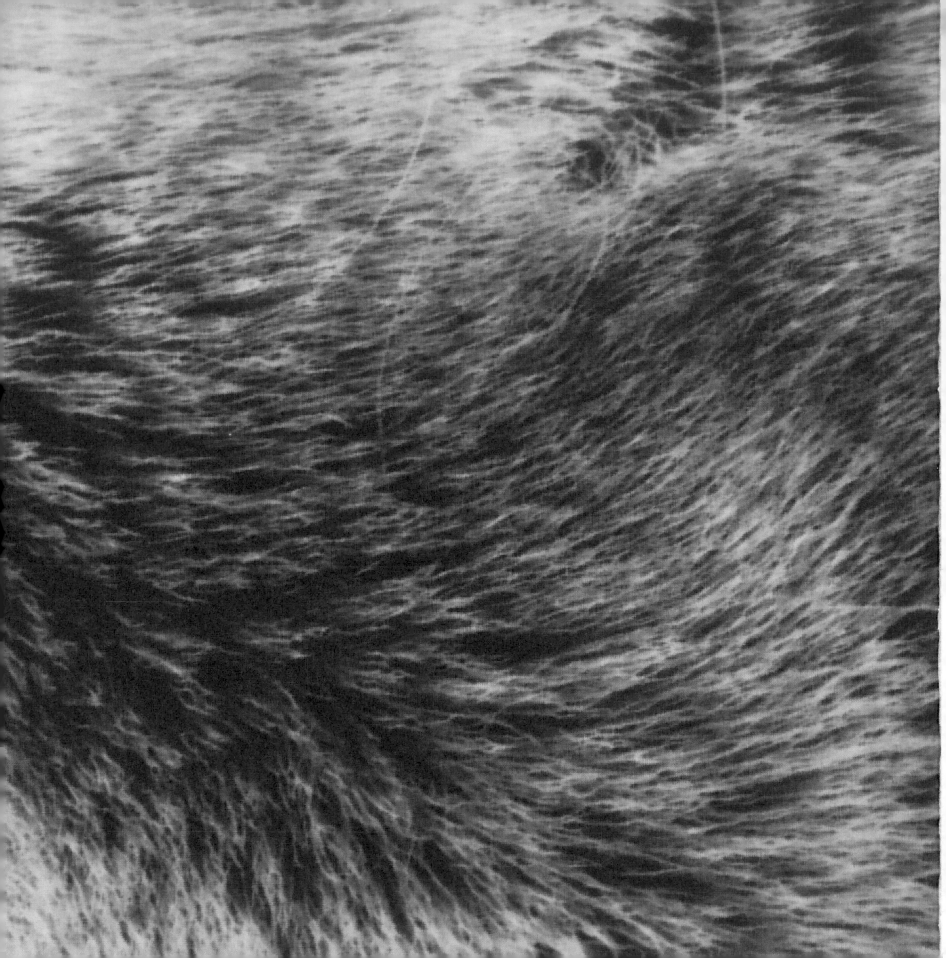

THEY LEAD

The Wolf Pack

Published by Familius LLC, www. Familius.com
PO Box 1249 Reedley, CA 93654

Familius books are available at special discounts,
whether for bulk purchases for sales promotions, or for family or corporate use.
For more information, email orders@familius.com

Library of Congress Control Number: 2022952156

Print ISBN 9781641709743
Ebook ISBN 9781641709248
KF 9781641709262
FE 9781641709255
Printed in China
Edited by Lacey Kupfer Wulf and Brooke Jorden
Book and cover design by Carlos Guerrero
Illustrations by Yumi Shimokawara

10 9 8 7 6 5 4 3 2 1
First Edition

THEY LEAD

The Wolf Pack

by June Smalls

Illustrated by Yumi Shimokawara

They are the leaders.
The creators of the pack.

Wolf packs are formed by a breeding pair that have left their family units to create their own. A pack is typically made up of parents, their offspring, and other non-breeding adults. A pack may be as few as two and has been recorded with up to 37.

Female gray wolves can be 60 to 100 pounds, and the males can be 70 to 145 pounds. While they are called gray wolves, their colors range from white to gray, brown, reddish, and black.

She digs the den, where their young will grow.

The female digs a den to birth her pups. The den will have a small opening and a large chamber in the rear. The female gives birth to between four to seven pups. Born deaf, blind, and defenseless, the pups will stay safely tucked in their den for about the first four weeks of their lives.

He patrols the territory and brings her food while she cares for the helpless pups.

The land in which the wolf pack lives and hunts is called a territory. This may span from 50 square miles to over 1,000 square miles. The wolves mark their territory with urine and scat (or dung) and other scent markers.

For the first five weeks of life, the pups rely on their mother's milk. As they start on solid food, the parents or older wolves will regurgitate meat for them to eat.

As seasons pass and new litters arrive, the pack grows and all work together to raise the young.

In a pack, typically only the breeding pair, sometimes called the alpha or dominant pair, will mate. Litters come in spring, and the young stay with the pack as long as there is enough food to sustain the size of the pack or until they strike out to find a mate and form their own packs.

The pups play under watchful eyes.

The breeding pair and the older wolves in the pack watch, feed, and protect the pups. Pups use play to build strength and practice hunting techniques. Play also helps strengthen pack bonds and brings them closer. The adults will join in the fun too.

They teach them the rules.
The pups must learn their
place in the pack.

The wolves' survival depends on the pack working together. A pack is organized and has rules.
It can look fierce at times, but the pack structure is important. The pack is led by the breeding
pair. Submissive wolves follow the direction of the higher-ranking dominant wolves.

Together they lead the hunt.
Together they feed.
Top dogs first.

The breeding pair leads the hunt with strength and cunning. The pack works as a team to bring down prey much larger than themselves. Chasing prey, they can reach speeds of up to 40 miles per hour.

Typically, the breeding pair will eat first, then other dominant wolves, and finally the submissive wolves eat last.

But they are not the top predator.
Sometimes wolves must retreat.

A fresh kill will attract the attention of other animals. Usually these scavengers are coyotes or ravens. Even an eagle may swoop in for an easy meal. Sometimes larger animals, such as a grizzly bear, will chase off the wolves, stealing their hard-earned meat for itself. The breeding pair will choose to fight or retreat for the safety of the pack.

The breeding pair sings. Their pack joins in. Howls ring through the sky calling for hunts, summoning their family, and warning others away.

Communication is vital to the wolf pack. They vocalize using howls, growls, barks, whimpers, and yips. Howls can be heard in the forests up to six miles and up to ten miles in open terrain.

Wolves also use scent marking and, most importantly, body language to communicate.

Fear or aggression is shown by baring teeth and flattening ears. Play is shown with bouncing and bowing. Submission is shown with crouched bodies, tail tucking, and even licking the muzzle of the dominant wolf.

Their songs can't always call everyone home.

The gray wolf has few natural predators. As with all wild animals, danger comes from old age, injury, and larger predators, like bears or mountain lions, and humans. Humans are especially dangerous to wolves, mostly due to wolf-livestock conflicts.

Their young pups grow.

A healthy, grown wolf eats about ten pounds of meat per day but often goes days in between meals. At times, they may gorge up to twenty pounds of meat at once when they have gone many days without food.

And hunt. And learn. And howl.
Before striking out on their own.

While they mostly hunt in packs for large prey, wolves will also eat smaller prey like beavers and hares, and wolves will even eat fruit such as berries, even though they are carnivores.

A wolf is mature between age two and three years old and may leave the pack.

The lone wolf finds a mate.
Together they form a new pack.

A lone wolf isn't usually alone for long. They wander, searching for a mate, a new territory, or a new pack. They may travel between 50 and 550 miles to find what they are looking for.

Together they sing.
Together they lead.

The newly mated pair will find an area to establish as their own territory. Their territory needs enough food to sustain the pack. Their journey will be difficult, and they will struggle, but wolves form packs, because they are stronger together.

"2020 Wolf Care Webinars Subscription." 2013. Wolf.org. Accessed 20 October 2020. https://wolf.org/wolf-info/basic-wolf-info/biology-and-behavior/communication/.

"2020 Wolf Care Webinars Subscription." 2013. Wolf.org. Accessed 20 October 2020. https://wolf.org/wolf-info/wild-kids/wolf-families/.

"Gray Wolf." The National Wildlife Foundation. Accessed 20 October 2020. https://www.nwf.org/en/Educational-Resources/Wildlife-Guide/Mammals/Gray-Wolf

"Gray Wolf." 2019. *National Geographic Kids*. 2019. https://kids.nationalgeographic.com/animals/mammals/gray-wolf/.

"Growing Up Wolf." *National Geographic*. Accessed 20 October 2020.   https://www.nationalgeographic.org/media/growing-up-wolf/

Nat Geo WILD. 2019. "Wolves 101 | Nat Geo Wild." YouTube. https://www.youtube.com/watch?v=YXMo5w9aMNs.

"River of No Return: Gray Wolf Fact Sheet" *Nature*. PBS. 21 October 2014. https://www.pbs.org/wnet/nature/river-of-no-return-gray-wolf-fact-sheet/7659/.

"Wolf Ecology Basics." 2017. U.S. National Park Service. 2017. https://www.nps.gov/articles/life-of-a-wolf.htm.

"Wolf." 2018. *National Geographic*. September 21, 2018. https://www.nationalgeographic.com/animals/mammals/g/gray-wolf/.

"Wolf Reproduction Biology and Maturation." *Western Wildlife Outreach*. Accessed 20 October 2020. http://westernwildlife.org/gray-wolf-outreach-project/biology-behavior-4/

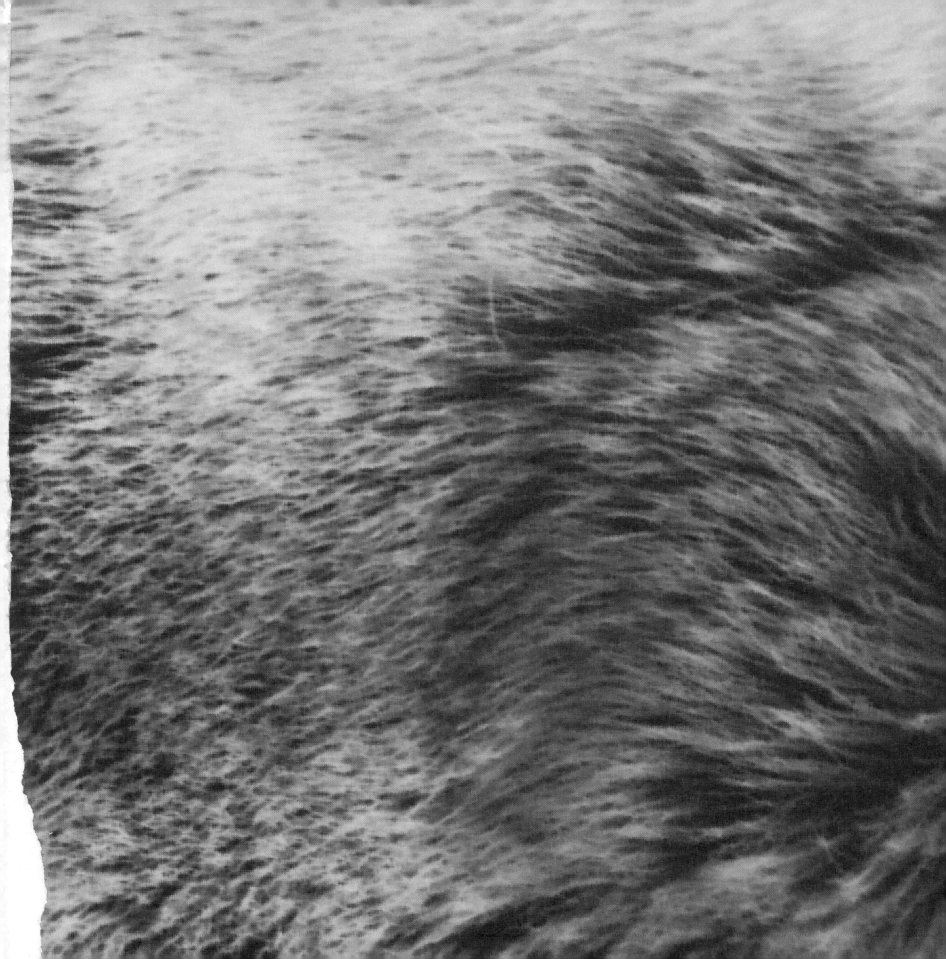

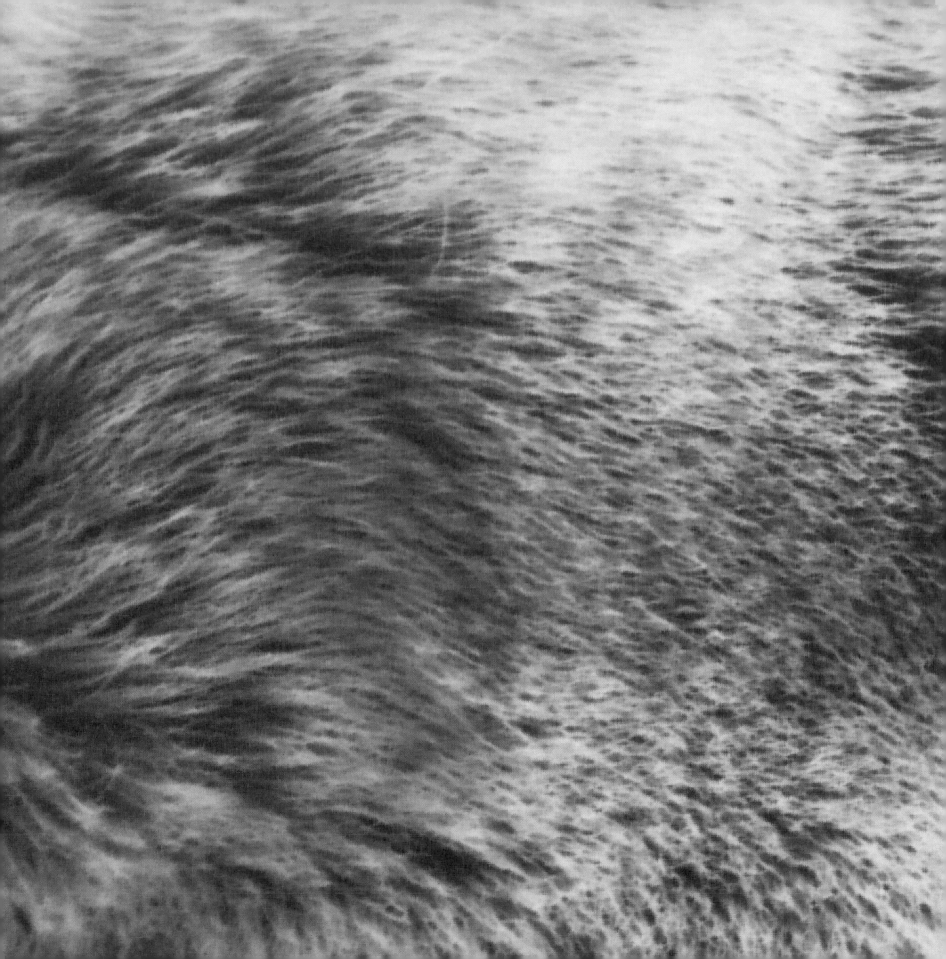